Allen

by Iain Gray

WRITING *to* REMEMBER

WRITING *to* REMEMBER

79 Main Street, Newtongrange,
Midlothian EH22 4NA
Tel: 0131 344 0414
E-mail: info@lang-syne.co.uk
www.langsyneshop.co.uk

Design by Dorothy Meikle
Printed by Printwell Ltd
© Lang Syne Publishers Ltd 2024

All rights reserved. No part of this publication may be reproduced, stored or introduced into a retrieval system, or transmitted in any form or by any means (electronic, mechanical, photocopying, recording or otherwise) without the prior written permission of Lang Syne Publishers Ltd.

ISBN 978-1-85217-775-1

Allen

MOTTO:
By faith and labour

CREST:
A collared hound

TERRITORIES include:
Shropshire

NAME variations include:
Alan
Allan
Alen
Allaine
Alleyn

Chapter one:

The origins of popular surnames

by George Forbes and Iain Gray

If you don't know where you came from, you won't know where you're going **is a frequently quoted observation and one that has a particular resonance today when there has been a marked upsurge in interest in genealogy, with increasing numbers of people curious to trace their family roots.**

Main sources for genealogical research include census returns and official records of births, marriages and deaths – and the key to unlocking the detail they contain is obviously a family surname, one that has been 'inherited' and passed from generation to generation.

No matter our station in life, we all have a surname – but it was not until about the middle of the fourteenth century that the practice of being identified by a particular surname became commonly established throughout the British Isles.

Previous to this, it was normal for a person to be identified through the use of only a forename.

But as population gradually increased and there were many more people with the same forename, surnames were adopted to distinguish one person, or community, from another.

Many common English surnames are patronymic in origin, meaning they stem from the forename of one's father – with 'Johnson,' for example, indicating 'son of John.'

It was the Normans, in the wake of their eleventh century conquest of Anglo-Saxon England, a pivotal moment in the nation's history, who first brought surnames into usage – although it was a gradual process.

For the Normans, these were names initially based on the title of their estates, local villages and chateaux in France to distinguish and identify these landholdings.

Such grand descriptions also helped enhance the prestige of these warlords and generally glorify their lofty positions high above the humble serfs slaving away below in the pecking order who had only single names, often with Biblical connotations as in Pierre and Jacques.

The only descriptive distinctions among the peasantry concerned their occupations, like 'Pierre the swineherd' or 'Jacques the ferryman.'

Roots of surnames that came into usage in England not only included Norman-French, but also Old French, Old Norse, Old English, Middle English, German, Latin, Greek, Hebrew and the Gaelic languages of the Celts.

The Normans themselves were originally Vikings, or 'Northmen', who raided, colonised and eventually settled down around the French coastline.

They had sailed up the Seine in their longboats in 900AD under their ferocious leader Rollo and ruled the roost in north eastern France before sailing over to conquer England in 1066 under Duke William of Normandy – better known to posterity as William the Conqueror, or King William I of England.

Granted lands in the newly-conquered England, some of their descendants later acquired territories in Wales, Scotland and Ireland – taking not only their own surnames, but also the practice of adopting a surname, with them.

But it was in England where Norman rule and custom first impacted, particularly in relation to the adoption of surnames.

This is reflected in the famous *Domesday Book*, a massive survey of much of England and Wales, ordered by William I, to determine who owned what, what it was worth and therefore how much they were liable to pay in taxes to the voracious Royal Exchequer.

Completed in 1086 and now held in the National Archives in Kew, London, 'Domesday' was an Old English word meaning 'Day of Judgement.'

This was because, in the words of one contemporary chronicler, "its decisions, like those of the Last Judgement, are unalterable."

It had been a requirement of all those English landholders – from the richest to the poorest – that they identify themselves for the purposes of the survey and for future reference by means of a surname.

This is why the *Domesday Book*, although written in Latin as was the practice for several centuries with both civic and ecclesiastical records, is an invaluable source for the early appearance of a wide range of English surnames.

Several of these names were coined in connection with occupations.

These include Baker and Smith, while Cooks, Chamberlains, Constables and Porters were to be found carrying out duties in large medieval households.

The church's influence can be found in names such as Bishop, Friar and Monk while the popular name of Bennett derives from the late fifth to mid-sixth century Saint Benedict, founder of the Benedictine order of monks.

The early medical profession is represented by Barber, while businessmen produced names that include Merchant and Sellers.

Down at the village watermill, the names that cropped up included Millar/Miller, Walker and Fuller, while other self-explanatory trades included Cooper, Tailor, Mason and Wright.

Even the scenery was utilised as in Moor, Hill, Wood and Forrest – while the hunt and the chase supplied names that include Hunter, Falconer, Fowler and Fox.

Colours are also a source of popular surnames, as in Black, Brown, Gray/Grey, Green and White, and would have denoted the colour of the clothing the person habitually wore or, apart from the obvious exception of 'Green', one's hair colouring or even complexion.

The surname Red developed into Reid, while

Blue was rare and no-one wanted to be associated with yellow.

Rather self-important individuals took surnames that include Goodman and Wiseman, while physical attributes crept into surnames such as Small and Little.

Many families proudly boast the heraldic device known as a Coat of Arms, as featured on our front cover.

The central motif of the Coat of Arms would originally have been what was borne on the shield of a warrior to distinguish himself from others on the battlefield.

Not featured on the Coat of Arms, but highlighted on page three, is the family motto and related crest – with the latter frequently different from the central motif.

Adding further variety to the rich cultural heritage that is represented by surnames is the appearance in recent times in lists of the 100 most common names found in England of ones that include Khan, Patel and Singh – names that have proud roots in the vast sub-continent of India.

Echoes of a far distant past can still be found in our surnames and they can be borne with pride in commemoration of our forebears.

Chapter two:

Invasion and civil war

Ranked 41st in some lists of the 100 most common surnames found in the United Kingdom today 'Allen', along with variants that include 'Alan' and 'Allan', is also a popular forename.

With a number of points of origin that include the Scottish and Irish-Gaelic 'Ailin', or 'Aluinn' – indicating 'little rock', 'harmony' or 'handsome', in common with many other surnames it was popularised in the wake of the Norman Conquest of 1066 – a key event in English history.

This popularity was through reverence for the fifth century St Alan of Quimper, in Brittany, many of whose followers had adopted the name and fought as Bretons in the ranks of William the Conqueror.

By 1066, England had become a nation with several powerful competitors to the throne.

In what were extremely complex family, political and military machinations, the king was the Anglo-Saxon Harold II, who had succeeded following the death of Edward the Confessor.

But his right to the kingship was contested by two powerful competitors – his brother-in-law King Harold Hardrada of Norway, in alliance with Tostig, Harold II's brother, and Duke William II of Normandy.

In what has become known as The Year of Three Battles, Hardrada invaded England and gained victory over the English king on September 20 at the battle of Fulford, in Yorkshire.

Five days later, however, Harold decisively defeated his brother-in-law and brother at the battle of Stamford Bridge.

But he had little time to celebrate his victory, having to immediately march south from Yorkshire to encounter a mighty invasion force, led by Duke William of Normandy that had landed at Hastings, in East Sussex.

Harold's battle-hardened but exhausted force of Anglo-Saxon soldiers confronted the Normans on October 14 in a battle subsequently depicted on the Bayeux tapestry – a 23ft long strip of embroidered linen thought to have been commissioned eleven years after the event by the Norman Odo of Bayeux.

Harold drew up a strong defensive position, at the top of Senlac Hill, building a shield wall to repel William's cavalry and infantry.

The Normans suffered heavy losses, but through a combination of the deadly skill of their archers and the ferocious determination of their cavalry they eventually won the day.

Anglo-Saxon morale had collapsed on the battlefield as word spread through the ranks that Harold had been killed – the Bayeux Tapestry depicting this as having happened when he was struck by an arrow.

Amidst the carnage of the battlefield, it was difficult to identify Harold – the last of the Anglo-Saxon kings.

Some sources assert William ordered his body to be thrown into the sea, while others state it was secretly buried at Waltham Abbey.

What is known with certainty, however, is that William in celebration of his great victory founded Battle Abbey, ordering that the altar be sited on the spot where Harold was believed to have fallen.

William was declared King of England on December 25, and the complete subjugation of his subjects followed.

Those Normans who had fought on his behalf were rewarded with the lands of Anglo-

Saxons, many of whom sought exile abroad as mercenaries.

Within an astonishingly short space of time, Norman manners, customs and law were imposed on England – laying the basis for what subsequently became established 'English' custom and practice.

Among the followers of William was the Breton warrior Alan fitz Flaad, whose descendants, having adopted the surname that later developed into the Anglicised form 'Allen', came to hold a family seat in the English county of Shropshire.

Born in 1105, William Fitz Alan was the wealthy landowner and stalwart supporter of King Henry I who, before his death in 1160, held the powerful and lucrative post of High Sheriff of Shropshire.

The Allen name features prominently in the historical record.

In the turbulent sixteenth century, William Allen was the Roman Catholic prelate who played a key role in the planning of the ultimately abortive Spanish Armada against British shores in 1588.

Born in 1532 at Rossall, near Fleetwood, Lancashire, he entered holy orders and became a canon at York Minster – and also a bitter opponent of Queen Elizabeth I, refusing to take the Oath of Supremacy that recognised the authority of the Protestant Church of England over the Roman Catholic Church.

This was at a time of murderous persecution against Catholics, and Allen was forced to seek refuge on the continent – although occasionally returning to his native shores to carry out clandestine work in opposition to Elizabeth.

In Rome, he established a college for the training of English priests, many of whom were fated to be martyred when they returned to England.

Founding the English College at Douai, Allen entered theological history by arranging the printing and publication of what became known as the *Douai-Rheims Bible*, after having relocated his college to Rheims, in France.

It was under the patronage of King Phillip II of Spain that he helped in the planning of the Spanish Armada, having described Queen Elizabeth I as "this woman hated by God and man."

Having been appointed a cardinal and de facto Archbishop of Canterbury before the doomed armada set sail, he died in 1594, while he is remembered to this day through a number of institutions that include the Venerable English College, Rome and the Cardinal Allen High School in his birthplace of Fleetwood.

Born in about 1583, Francis Allen was the politician and financier who figures in the historical record of the English Civil War as a 'regicide', having been complicit in the decision to execute King Charles I.

The king had incurred the wrath of Parliament by his insistence on the 'divine right' of monarchs, and added to this was Parliament's fear of Catholic 'subversion' against the state and Charles' stubborn refusal to grant demands for religious and constitutional concessions.

Matters came to a head with the outbreak of the Civil War in 1642, with Parliamentary forces, known as the New Model Army and commanded by Oliver Cromwell and Sir Thomas Fairfax, arrayed against the Royalist army of the king.

In what became an increasingly bloody and complex conflict, spreading to Scotland and Ireland and with rapidly shifting loyalties on both sides, the 49-year-old king was eventually captured, put on trial and executed in January of 1649 on the orders of Parliament.

Elected in 1642 to what was known as the Long Parliament for the constituency of Cockermouth, Francis Allen had been one of the 135 commissioners who had sat in judgement at the king's trial.

Although not a signatory to the monarch's death warrant, as a commissioner he was posthumously deemed, following the Restoration of King Charles II in 1660, to have been a regicide (the action of killing a king).

He died two years before the Restoration, with his family paying the price for his role in the king's execution when, being excluded from the terms of the 1660 Act of Indemnity, his estates were confiscated.

Chapter three:

Honours and distinction

Bearers of the Allen name and its popular spelling variant 'Allan' have gained renown through a wide and colourful range of endeavours and pursuits, including the sciences.

Born the son of a sailmaker in Spitalfields, London in 1770, William Allen was the pharmacist and philanthropist who, in 1841, co-founded what is today's prestigious Royal Pharmaceutical Society.

A friend and contemporary of fellow scientists John Dalton and Humphry Davy, he carried out pioneering research into the properties of carbon, while as an entrepreneur he co-founded a pharmaceutical business in London, Allen and Hanburys'.

A follower of the Quaker religious faith, he gifted a great deal of his wealth to a number of causes that included the establishment of an agricultural settlement in Lindfield, Sussex.

This was in a bid to alleviate poverty at a time when many were forced to seek new lives for themselves in foreign lands, particularly North

America, and Allen's idea was to create what became known as 'Colonies of Home', such as Lindfield.

Also a prominent member of the Society for the Abolition of the Slave Trade, he died in 1843, while the company he co-founded today forms part of the pharmaceutical group Glaxo Laboratories.

A pioneer in the fields of quantum theory and X-rays, Herbert Allen was the English physicist born in 1873 in Bodmin, Cornwall.

The son of a Welsh Methodist minister, he studied at a number of institutions that include Trinity College, Cambridge, later specialising in early X-ray research and what was then the fledgling and highly complex field of quantum theory.

Also having been involved in research into spectral photography and having worked for a time in the laboratories of Edinburgh University, he died in 1954.

Bearers of the Allen name have also gained distinction in battle.

Born in 1844, William Allen was an English recipient of the Victoria Cross (VC), the highest award for gallantry in the face of enemy action for British and Commonwealth forces.

He had been serving with the 2nd Battalion, 24th Regiment of Foot, during the Zulu Wars, when the regiment came under attack at Rorke's Drift, Natal, in January of 1879.

Allen, who had been reduced from the rank of sergeant to corporal for being drunk on duty, won his VC for helping to evacuate wounded comrades from the base hospital; he died in 1890.

In a later conflict, yet another William Allen was a recipient of the VC.

Born in Sheffield in 1892, he was a captain in the Royal Army Medical Corps (RAMC) during the First World War when, in September of 1916 near Mesnil, in France, he ignored very heavy shellfire and his own injuries to tend wounded comrades.

He died in 1933, while his VC is now on display in the British Army Medical Museum, Aldershot.

Taking to the skies, Captain Charles Allen was the British First World War flying ace credited with shooting down seven Fokker D. VIIs over a six-month period in 1918.

This was as a Sopwith Camel pilot attached to 2014 Squadron RAF, while on aerial combat duty over the Western Front.

Born in Liverpool in 1899, he died in 1974, the recipient of a number of honours and awards that include Belgium's Knight of the Order of the Crown and also the nation's Croix de Guerre.

With the popular spelling variant 'Allan', one of the wealthiest men in the world and the richest man in Canada at the time of his death in 1882, Sir Hugh Allan was the entrepreneur born in 1810 in Saltcoats, North Ayrshire.

His father, Alexander Allan, born in 1780 and a first cousin of Scotland's national bard Robert Burns, began his working life as a carpenter on an estate at Fairlie, in Ayrshire.

He later became the master of a small ship, or brig, laying the foundation of the Allan Shipping Line, running goods from the Scottish west coast port of Greenock to Montreal, and returning with Canadian goods.

Hugh Allan began working for his father in 1823, but three years later went to work in Montreal for the grain merchant William Kerr, one of his father's business partners.

By 1835, he had become a partner in the Montreal importing firm of Millar, Edmonstone and Co; eventually taking over its shipping operation with the financial backing of his family back in Scotland.

Later joined by his brother Andrew, he soon added to the Allan Shipping Line with his Montreal Ocean Steamship Company, which had the lucrative contract to take mail to and from Montreal to London and to and from Montreal to the American port of Portland, in Maine.

Meanwhile another brother, James, had taken over from his father, running the Allan Shipping Line's Greenock base, while another brother, Bryce, was in charge of the company's Liverpool base.

The ever-enterprising Hugh Allan also branched out into railways, and by the 1870s had created a syndicate to build Canada's national railway.

Also a director of the Bank of Montreal, he was knighted by Queen Victoria in 1871, eleven years before his death.

From the world of commerce to the world of political activism, Alfred Allen, more formally known as Baron Allen of Fallowfield, was the British trades unionist born in Bristol in 1914.

Having held a number of trades union posts that included national officer of the Union of Shop,

Distributive Workers and election as president in 1974 of the Trades Union Congress (TUC), he also later served as a member of the Board of Governors of the BBC.

He died in 1985, ten years after having been elevated to the Peerage as Baron Allen of Fallowfield, of Fallowfield, in Greater Manchester.

Chapter four:

On the world stage

Born in 1935 in The Bronx, New York City and raised in Brooklyn, Allan Stewart Konisberg is the multitalented American actor, stand-up comedian, screenwriter, director and jazz clarinettist better known as Woody Allen.

The son of a jewellery engraver and waiter and a bookkeeper of Russian-Jewish roots, he began writing jokes when aged 15 – some of which were accepted by comedians who included Phil Silvers and Sid Caeser.

Joining the NBC Writers' Development Program when he was aged 19, he later wrote for the NBC *Comedy Hour*, *The Tonight Show* and *The Ed Sullivan Show*.

Changing his name to Heywood Allen and then to Woody Allen, and also having written gags for Bob Hope – who described him as "half a genius" – and performing as a stand-up comedian in his own right, in 1965 he wrote the screenplay for *What's New Pussycat?*

Co-writing, acting and directing the 1969

Take the Money and Run, he followed this with a string of box-office hits that include the 1972 *Everything You Always Wanted to Know About Sex*, the 1973 *Sleeper* and, from 1975, *Love and Death*.

One of his most successful films is the 1977 *Annie Hall*, for which Diane Keaton – who has starred in a number of other Allen films – won an Academy Award for Best Actress in a Leading Role and Allen won the awards for Best Picture, Best Original Screenplay and Best Director.

Ranked at No. 35 in the American Film Institute's "100 Best Movies" and at No. 4 in its list of "100 Best Comedies", it has been followed by other notable films. These include the 1979 black-and-white *Manhattan*, the 1986 *Hannah and her Sisters* the 2005 *Match Point*, the 2016 *Café Society* and, from 2019, *A Rainy Day in New York*.

Elected a Fellow of the American Academy of Arts and Sciences in 2001, Allen was romantically involved for a time with Diane Keaton and the actress Stacy Nelkin, while he has been married thrice.

It was in 1979 that he married his third wife, Soon-Yi Previn, the adopted daughter of actress Mia Farrow, with whom he had a twelve-year relationship, and her former husband the composer André Previn.

In 2020, employees of the Hatchette Book Group walked-out in protest over plans by the company to publish Allen's autobiography *Apropos of Nothing*, because of controversy over his private life and claims of abuse by his adopted daughter Dylan Farrow.

Hatchette returned the rights to the book to Allen and it was subsequently published by Arcade Publishing.

Known as the comedy partner of her real-life husband George Burns in the *Burns and Allen* radio and television shows, **Gracie Allen** was the American comedienne of Irish descent born in San Francisco in 1895.

First taking to the stage with her three sisters as The Four Colleens and performing Irish folk dances, she was aged seventeen when she met Burns and formed a vaudeville comedy act, marrying four years later.

Stars of their own radio and television shows until Gracie retired in 1958, the couple also appeared in the 1930s in screen productions that include the 1934 W.C. Fields film *Six of a Kind* and, with Fred Astaire, in the 1937 *A Damsel in Distress*.

Following his wife's retirement, Burns, who

died in 1996 aged 100, carried on for a time with *The George Burns Show*, while Gracie – who unusually had two different coloured eyes, one green and one blue – had died in 1963.

The recipient of a star on the Hollywood Walk of Fame, she is also honoured through The Grace Award, presented annually by the Alliance for Women in Media in recognition of excellence in fields that include comedy, drama, documentary and news.

On the contemporary stage, **Debbie Allen** is the American actress, dancer and choreographer best known for her role of dance teacher Lydia Grant in the 1980 film *Fame* and its television adaptation of the same name from 1982 to 1987.

A three-time Emmy Award winner for the series – for which she was the main choreographer – she also appears in the 2009 film remake of *Fame*.

Born in 1950 in Houston, Texas, as a leading stage actress she is the recipient of a Tony Award nomination and a Drama Desk Award for her performance in the Broadway revival of *West Side Story* and another nomination for her role in the musical *Raisin*.

Also having appeared in the 1979 television mini-series *Roots: The Next Generation*, she is the recipient of a star on the Hollywood Walk of Fame and a George and Ira Gershwin Award for Lifetime Musical Achievement.

Born in 1951 in Carrollton, Illinois of a rich mix of English, Scottish, Welsh and Irish descent, **Karen Allen** is the American actress whose screen credits include the role of Marion Ravenwood in the 1981 *Raiders of the Lost Ark* and in the 2008 *Indiana Jones and the Kingdom of the Crystal Skull*, the 1988 *Scrooged* and, from 2000, *The Perfect Storm*.

On British shores, **Sheila Allen**, born in 1932, was the actress best known for her role of Cassie Manson in the television drama series *Bouquet of Barbed Wire* and its sequel, from 1976 to 1977, *Another Bouquet*.

A member of the Royal Shakespeare Company from 1966 to 1978 and with big screen credits that include the 1963 *Children of the Damned*, the 2003 *Love Actually* and, from 2005, *Harry Potter and the Goblet of Fire*, she died in 2011.

A child actress of both stage and screen, **Isabelle Allen** was born in 2002 in Salisbury, Wiltshire.

Best known for her role of Cosette in the screen adaptation of *Les Misérables*, she won the Young Artist Award for Best Supporting Actress Age

Ten and Under, while having reprised the role in a West End Stage production, she also played the role of Brigitta Von Trap in a 2013 production of *The Sound of Music*.

Born in Lancashire in 1965, **Fiona Allen** is the actress and comedienne whose television credits include the comedy series *Smack the Pony* and *Goodness Gracious Me*.

Also having appeared in the soap *Coronation Street* and the sitcom *Happiness*, she is married to Michael Parkinson, son of the former television chat show host of the same name.

Known for his role of gang leader Buzz Gunderson in the 1955 *Rebel Without a Cause*, starring James Dean, **Corey Allen** was the American actor, television and film writer, director and producer born Alan Cohen in 1934 in Cleveland, Ohio.

Having directed television shows that include *The Rockford Files*, *Ironside* and *Hill Street Blues* – for which he won an Emmy Award in 1984 – he died in 2010.

A comedian and satirist, David Tynan O'Mahony, better known to television audiences by his stage name of **Dave Allen**, was born in Dublin in 1936.

Known for his British television show *Dave Allen at Large* throughout the late 1960s, 1970s and again the late 1980s and early 1990s, he was popular for his wry wit and sardonic sense of humour.

With the show interspersed with sketches, he delivered witty monologues while seated and occasionally smoking and sipping from a glass of whisky. Unknown to television viewers, however, the 'whisky' was actually ginger ale.

Also known for his 'sign-off' to the show of "Goodnight, thank you, and may your God go with you", he died in 2005.

Born in 1953 in Swansea, Wales, **Keith Allen** is the actor, comedian and presenter whose many television credits include *The Comic Strip Presents* and *Martin Chuzzlewit*.

Also having played the role of the Sheriff of Nottingham from 2006 to 2009 in *Robin Hood*, he is the father of the singer **Lily Allen**.

Born in London in 1985, her 2006 album *Alright Still* won nominations for a number of awards including a Grammy and the BRIT Awards, while she hosted the talk show *Lily Allen and Friends*.

Behind the camera lens, **Irwin Allen** was the American television and film director known as the

"Master of Disaster" for his work in the disaster movie genre.

Born in New York City in 1916 he died in 1991, with credits that include the 1972 *The Poseidon Adventure* and, from 1974, *The Towering Inferno*.

An award-winning British television and film producer and executive, **Kenton Allen** was born in Wolverhampton in 1965.

Joining the BBC when he was aged 18 as a trainee studio manager, he went on to become chief executive of Big Talk Productions in 2008 and is credited with work on productions that include the BAFTA award-winning sitcoms *The Royle Family* and *Rev.*, and the 2007 film *Shooter*, for which he won a 2005 BAFTA Award.

Born in London in 1944, **Dick Allen** was the highly acclaimed film editor who received the 1986 BAFTA Award for Best Film Editor for *Hotel du Lac* and the 1991 award for the television mini-series *Portrait of a Marriage*. Also having worked on television documentary drama series that include *The Tribal Eye*, he died in 2007.

Bearers of the Allen name have also excelled in the highly competitive world of sport.

In the rough and tumble of the rugby pitch,

Andy Allen, born in 1967 in Newport, is the Welsh international rugby union footballer who played for his nation as a lock, while **Anthony Allen** formerly played as a centre for Leicester Tigers.

Born in Southampton in 1986, he made his international debut, against New Zealand, in 2006, while he was a member of the England Saxons squads in both 2008 and 2010 that won the Churchill Cup in Canada/America.

In the creative world of the written word, **Walter Allen** was the noted twentieth century English literary critic and novelist born in 1911 in Aston, Birmingham.

A member of the Birmingham Group of authors, his works include the 1938 *Drowned* and, from 1981, his autobiographical *As I Walked Down New Grub Street*; also literary editor for a time of the *New Statesman*, he died in 1995.

In the world of music, Christopher Allen, better known as **Daevid Allen**, was the Australian guitarist, singer, composer and poet who, after settling in England in 1966, founded the progressive rock band Soft Machine.

Born in Melbourne in 1938 and also founder of the band Gong, he died in 2015.

One contemporary musician with a rather unusual claim to fame is the English hard rock drummer **Rick Allen**.

Born in 1963 in Dronfield, Derbyshire he was aged 15 when he joined the band Def Leppard, enjoying chart success with albums that include the 1981 *High 'n' Dry*, the 1999 *Euphoria* and, from 2008, *Songs from the Sparkle Lounge*.

But his career appeared to have come to an untimely end in 1984 when his left arm was severed in a road accident.

Surgeons managed to re-attach the arm, but it had to be re-amputated when infection set in.

Undaunted, and with the help of engineers, he designed a drum kit that allowed him to play some drum rhythms while later, with the encouragement and help of Status Quo drummer Jeff Rich, an even more sophisticated kit was designed to accommodate his disability.

With Def Leppard still enjoying international chart success and Allen known to fans as "The Thunder God", he and his wife are co-founders of The Raven Drum Foundation – a charity set up to help disabled veterans and others through 'healing arts' programmes.